Fisher-Price® LittlePeople®

Alphabet Farm

Modern Publishing
A Division of Unisystems, Inc.
New York, New York 10022
Series UPC Number: 19615

W9-BLQ-729

Modern Publishing
A Division of Unisystems, Inc.
New York, New York 10022
Printed in Canada

The farm's a good place for an alphabet game.
You'll find a word for any letter you name.

A is for **apples** that grow on a tree.
The **barn**, where the animals live, starts with **B**.

C is for **cow**, a big gentle beast.
She moos as she nibbles a grassy green feast.

The **dairy**, where **Daisy** gives milk, starts with **D**,
And **eggs** that are laid by the hens start with **E**.

F is for **farmer**. His tractor's **four**-wheeled.
He can **fix** up a **fence** or work in the **field**.

G is for **goats**; at the **gate** they are found.
H is for **horns**, good for kidding around.

I is for **ice cream**, a great homemade treat.
J is for **jelly**, from berries so sweet.

K is for **kitty**, who scares mice away.
L is for **lambs**, who frolic all day.

M is for **milking**, when **Mabel** says "**MOO!**"
N is for **nesting**. The lovebirds say "coo."

O is for **oats**, a good meal for a horse.
P is for **pigs** in a **puddle**, of course!

Q is for **quilt**, hanging out on the line.
R is for **rooster**, who greets the sunshine.
S is a **saddle** for Pony to wear.
He's happy to carry me everywhere!

Tools and **tractor** start with **T**.
How's the engine? We'll soon see.

U is for **up** in the hayloft so high.
Under the roof, there's a lot we can spy.

V is for **vine**, and **vane** that points east.
W's for **wagon**. The **wheels** are all greased.

X marks the spot where our ride will begin.
Giddyup, tractor, we're off for a spin!

Y is for the bright **yellow** stars in the sky.
Z is for the shooting stars as they go **zooming** by.

Now we're back home, and snug in our beds,
And alphabet dreams are filling our heads.